Building Confidence for Kids

How to build self esteem in your child (parent guide).

Yaw Sweet, 2022.

Table of Contents

Foreword

In the formative years of a child's life, confidence development is crucial. It is significant because your child will need it to get through many challenges in life. It is the parent's responsibility to assist their child in developing self-confidence. There are numerous ways you can support your kid's confidence-building.

Increasing your child's self-confidence will help them feel good about themselves and will also help them get ready for the future. What can I do to help my child have more self-confidence, you may wonder?The solution is simple, and you can take a number of daily actions that will benefit you and only take a short amount of time.

You can learn more about the value of boosting your self-confidence and how to do it in these books you are about to read. Building your child's confidence will be much easier if you pay close attention and soak up all the information in these books.

Introduction

When you think about a child with confidence, one who can stand in front of others and give a speech without trembling, one who is not afraid to speak their mind. someone who is good at making and keeping friends. However, this isn't always the case; frequently, we struggle to give our children the things we want for them.

There are probably a lot of things that, if you are new to parenting, you are not entirely sure how to do. One of them might be the significance of or methods for fostering confidence in your child. Lack of confidence can be a result of many things. Therefore, It can be overcome, just like every other challenge you have faced in life. Building your child's self-confidence will be as simple as a stroll in the park if you just pick up a few helpful tricks and set aside some extra time for them.

Chapter 1:

The Fundamentals of Confidence

The Fundamentals

The degree of confidence a person had as a child has a significant impact on their level of confidence as an adult. This is one of the main reasons it's so crucial to give your child a healthy dose of confidence. Your child will develop this important life skill with a little bit of time and effort. As a parent, you'll need to take care of a few things. These are a few instances:

Always Make Time:

No matter how busy you are, you must always find time for your child! A great way to develop a child's self-confidence and sense of worth is to demonstrate that they come first in your household. Taking the time to plan activities with your child that can aid in the process of boosting their confidence is advised. This might entail taking them somewhere they can practice what they are good at or even somewhere they can try something new. This will demonstrate their talent, which is a terrific confidence builder. One illustration would be taking a kid to the park to play ball.If your child isn't interested in sports, take them to a gathering where they can demonstrate their knowledge of various topics, and never forget to express your admiration.

Don't Be Too Tough:
It's important not to be too gentle with your child, but it's also crucial not to be too harsh. On the other hand, being too strict will probably result in low self-confidence because a child will feel as though they never do anything right. Being too easy on your child will probably not instill proper morals in a child or teach them to be responsible. As a parent, you must strike a balance and apply discipline equally to all children. It's important to try different parenting approaches to see which ones

work best for your particular child in order to develop their self-confidence.

Set a Good Example:
 It is your responsibility as a parent to set a good example and serve as a role model for your child. Your level of self-confidence is one of the personality traits that your child will most likely pick up from you. It is critical that you always appear to have control of the situation and that you have complete faith in yourself. Also, never criticize yourself in front of your child, as this will most likely encourage them to do the same.

Beware of Bullies:
Bullying is becoming more common. This is most likely due to the fact that, thanks to social media, children can bully one another at any time and from any location. Bullying is probably one of the quickest ways to destroy a child's self-esteem. Bullies frequently have low self-esteem and, in

order to make themselves feel better, try to undermine the confidence of others. This is why you must be on the lookout for signs that your child is being bullied and intervene immediately! Here are some examples of behaviors your child may exhibit while being bullied:

- **Suddenly don't want to go to school**
- **Depression**
- **Fear of Anxiety**
- **Less Social Interactions**
- **Not Appearing Like Themselves**
- **Refusing to Discuss Their School Day**

If you notice any of these signs, you must act immediately!

Chapter 2:

Make it clear to your child that you believe in them.

Let your child know that you believe in them. Actually, completing this task is very easy and doesn't take much effort. Nevertheless, it is still crucial. You can let your child know that you believe in them in a variety of ways. You can find activities that significantly boost your child's self-assurance while demonstrating your belief in them with enough time and effort. Showing your child that you believe in them can be accomplished in a variety of ways. What works for one child may not have the same effect on another. This means you'll most likely have to experiment until you find something that works. If you're not sure where to begin, here are a few ideas:

Encourage Your Child to Try New Things

Encouraging your child to try new things is a great way to boost their confidence and demonstrate that you fully believe in their ability to succeed. Pay attention to what your child says, especially when it comes to things they want to do but don't think they can.

Encourage them to try as a way to demonstrate your belief in them in this circumstance. Inform them that you have faith in them and that anything is possible for them if they put their minds to it. It is crucial to convey to them that while they might not be exceptionally good at something when they first begin, with time and practice, they will improve greatly.

Push them outside of their comfort zone

A child's chances of developing self-confidence are much lower than those of a child who is constantly challenging themselves. Teaching your child to take on challenges will significantly boost their self-confidence and demonstrate to them that you have faith in their abilities.

Praise Your Child

Praising your child can help them feel more confident and know that you have faith in them. This is particularly true if the boasting is done in their presence. Telling others about their successes and what you anticipate they will accomplish in the future will undoubtedly increase their confidence. However, be careful not to boast excessively lest the kid grow arrogant.

Chapter 3

Praise Their Successes, Understand Their Fears

Helping your child build a healthy level of self-confidence requires acknowledging noboth their accomplishments and their fears. This is particularly true when a kid overcomes their fear to complete a task. It is crucial to keep in mind that every small success should be celebrated when attempting to boost a child's confidence. No matter how small the task, your child will gain a lot from your praise for their success.

In this chapter, we'll discuss two aspects of a parent's responsibility: praising their child's accomplishments and comprehending their child's fears. It's critical for parents to realize that both are equally crucial to the process of establishing confidence in their child. First, we will discuss the significance of and methods for recognizing a child's accomplishments.

Praise Their Successes

Praise your child's successes, no matter how insignificant they may seem to you, as this is essential for fostering confidence. Your child will feel good about themselves and develop self-confidence as a result of feeling as though they are constantly doing things that impress you.

In fact, praising your child's accomplishments can lead to more positive results than consistently calling attention to any bad behavior your child might exhibit. This is not surprising because constantly calling attention to what a child does incorrectly makes them feel as though they are incapable of doing anything right. Conversely, only praising your child's successes and refusing to discuss their errors with them will have detrimental effects. This is due to the fact that the kid will think they can do no wrong. Finding a sound balance between criticizing errors and praising successes is crucial. You must be careful not to spoil or over-treat your child when praising their accomplishments. Your child will logically come to believe that this will happen every time they do something if you give them a sizable reward every time they finish a small task. When the rewards stop, the child may behave badly because they won't understand why they no longer get a reward for performing a particular task. It is suggested that rewards be saved for more significant achievements. A verbal commendation or a pat on the back will do just fine for smaller accomplishments.

Recognize Your Child's Fears

Recognizing your child's fears is important for the growth of your child's self-confidence. How can fear increase my child's self-confidence, you may be wondering. The answer is the fact that overcoming fear can boost a person's self-confidence dramatically. While trying to overcome fears it is important that you first understand them. You do not want to set your child up for failure. Some of the things they may be scared to attempt may actually be too difficult for them. One of the worst things you can do while trying to build a child's confidence is put them in a situation where they will not win. You should talk to your child to find out what they are afraid of doing and decide whether it would be wise to encourage them to face those fears.

Once you understand your child's fears and have determined the possible negative and positive outcomes of facing them, you may make the decision to motivate your child to face those fears. Accomplishing a task that a child once feared they would fail is probably one of the best ways to build their self-confidence. This is because the process demonstrates to them that, if they set their minds to something, they can accomplish anything, no matter how difficult or terrifying it may seem.

It's crucial to avoid pressuring your child to confront too many of their fears. If you push your child too hard, the outcome might not be what you had in mind. The child might become anxious, which might affect how they feel for the rest of their lives. This could actually undermine their confidence further because their anxiety might prevent them from completing other tasks that they once completed without any trouble.

Chapter 4:
Teach Them to Learn From Mistakes

No one in our world is perfect, so everyone occasionally makes mistakes and errors. The most crucial thing is that we learn to grow as individuals and draw lessons from our errors. We must then use these lessons to keep us from making future mistakes of a similar type. It is all part of the growing process. It is the same for a child who needs to build their self-confidence.

More recently than you, your child has been a part of this world. Therefore, it only makes sense that you are in charge of imparting to your child the ability to learn from mistakes. You, as a parent, have undoubtedly encountered this situation numerous times and have much more experience with it than your child does. No one is perfect, as was previously mentioned, and everyone makes mistakes. Whether a person learns from their mistakes or not determines whether they succeed or fail in life.

Building your child's self-confidence is possible through success and success is possible through your child learning from their mistakes. You must teach your child not to be too hard on themselves or beat themselves up when they make a mistake.

You must teach them to look at the situation from a logical standpoint and determine the things that they could have done different in order to get a more desirable outcome. You will be surprised at how much this will boost your child's self-confidence. This process will mature your child's thinking process and they will be more confident because they will know that even if they do not succeed at something the first time, they will determine their mistakes, try again and succeed.

Failure to teach your child about learning from their mistakes will eventually have a negative impact on their self-confidence. If your child does not learn from their mistakes, they will most likely repeat them. This can make a child feel stuck in a rut or as if success is out of reach. They will feel as if they can't do anything, and their motivation to live will gradually dwindle. Most people in correctional institutions, whether adult or juvenile, are a perfect example of this. Most of the people there will tell you that they were never taught the importance of learning from their mistakes. These people continued to make the same mistakes until they felt as if life was hopeless and completely gave up on trying to be successful. You do not want this happen to your child. In order for you to avoid a situation like this you must teach your child the importance of learning from their errors.

Chapter 5:
Accept Your Child for Who He or She Is

There might be some characteristics of your child that you wish were different. The fact is that your child cannot change some aspects of themselves. You cannot hold your child responsible for who they are because you chose to give them life; they did not ask to enter this world. You may not agree with some of the things your child does in their daily life, but you must accept them as facts and work to change the behaviors.

The following are some examples of types of things your child cannot change about themselves.

Sexuality

This is probably the area where the largest number of parents have a hard time accepting their child for who they are. This may be due to moral stand points or it may be due to religious backgrounds and personal beliefs. No matter what the reason is, you must learn to accept your child for who they are. Showing your child that you love them for who they are will greatly improve their self-confidence and make them feel much better about themselves. Apart from this, trying to force your child to change something about themselves such as sexuality will cause many difficulties for a child in life. They will most likely become confused about who they truly are and this will surely destroy their future and confidence.

Likes and Dislikes

You have to learn to accept your child's likes, dislikes, and interests. You have to understand that just because you want your son to grow up to be a football player or your daughter to be a beauty queen does not mean they want the same for their life. You need to encourage your child to do the things they like in life, even if they do not adhere to your set dreams and goals of your child. After all, it is their life and they are the one who has to live it, parents are just passengers on the journey used as guidance.

Accept Your Child's Strengths and Weaknesses

It's important for you as a parent to realize that not every expectation you have for your child will be met. You need to keep in mind to set reasonable expectations for your child and to show patience if they fall short of them. If you constantly express disapproval when a child falls short of one of your expectations, you will undermine the child's self-esteem and cause them to feel inferior or unworthy. By demonstrating to your child that you will accept them as long as they put forth their best effort in everything they do, you will undoubtedly increase their self-assurance and help them live a happier and more prosperous life.

These are just a few of the many things that you may eventually have to accept about your child. You do not have to agree with everything your child does, as was previously stated, but it is crucial that you learn to accept it for your own wellbeing as well as your child's.

Chapter 6:

Make an effort to be involved in your child's life and to provide opportunities for positive growth

If you want your child to be confident and successful, you must be actively involved in their life and provide opportunities for growth while they are growing. This step really only requires spending time with your child. Do some fun activities with your child and use this time to learn more about their lives. The more you understand about what is going on in your child's life, the better you will be able to assist them in developing confidence.

As a parent, you must ensure that you are involved in your child's life. This does not mean only when it is convenient for you; it means always, even when it is difficult. You might have to do things you don't want to do or go to events you don't want to go to. It makes no difference; you must participate.

Being involved in your child's life demonstrates to them that you genuinely care about them while also increasing their self-worth and self-confidence.

You should ask your child about their life and how they feel things are going for them. During these conversations, you should try to identify the areas where you can support them in gaining confidence and creating new opportunities for them. The perfect time to do this would be at dinner, when the entire family is seated at the table rather than in front of the TV on the couch. While it's important to engage with your child's interests and try to be more involved in their lives, you also need to set aside specific family times for everyone to spend time together. This greatly strengthens the bonds between family members and increases the likelihood that your child will confide in you about their experiences. When your child is honest with you, they will tell you what is preventing them from succeeding, which will enable you to help them regain their confidence.

You must exercise extra caution to avoid meddling too deeply in your child's life. If you try to meddle too much in your child's life, they might feel like you are trying to take over or control their life. Remember that this is their life, and even though you might disagree with some of their choices, you must let them grow up on their own. The key to a happy family and a confident child is to be involved in your child's life to a healthy degree without trying to take over their life.

Chapter 7:

Why Is It Important to Delegate Responsibilities?

Life's responsibilities are crucial for a child, especially when it comes to boosting their self-esteem. You must be reasonable when assigning your child tasks because you do not want to condemn them to failure. Setting tasks that are too challenging could lead to failure, which would further damage your child's confidence. On the other hand, a child who correctly fulfills their duties will be given greater self-confidence. Therefore, it is suggested that you begin with small tasks and progress to bigger ones once the smaller ones can be completed with ease.

Children should be given simple chores like making their bed and cleaning their room as their first responsibilities. You might want to start adding more duties after they can manage this on a daily basis, like doing the dishes a few times a week or vacuuming the carpet. Making a child's responsibilities harder as they get older and become more capable is necessary. Getting your child a pet is one suggestion that might work. It's best to get something smaller than a dog because most people are unaware of how much upkeep a dog actually requires. Starting with an animal, like a hamster or some fish, might be preferable. Your child will grow more responsible as a result of having to take care of this animal's needs while also having to feed it every day. By successfully completing their duties, they will also gain more self-confidence because they will realize that they are capable of accomplishing difficult tasks.

It will be difficult at first to instill responsibilities in your child's daily life, but with perseverance and effort it will be successful in boosting your child's confidence.

Chapter 8:
The Drawbacks of Low Self-Confidence

A child who lacks self-confidence will undoubtedly face a lot more difficulties in life than a child who is confident. When a person has high self-confidence, they develop positive character traits, whereas when they have low self-confidence, they develop negative traits. Having low levels of confidence has a wide range of negative effects. These drawbacks may significantly harm a person's present and future circumstances. Because of this, it is crucial to instill in your child a strong sense of self-worth at a young age. The following are some instances of the detrimental effects low self-confidence can have on a child:

Fearful of Trying New Things

If your child lacks self-confidence, they may find it challenging to try new things. They will repeatedly succumb to their fear of failing. This fear will stop them dead in their tracks every time they think of trying to do something new.

Bad Social Impacts

If your child suffers from low self-confidence they will likely experience difficulty with their social life in the future. A task as simple as approaching someone to say hello can feel impossible if a person has low self-confidence. In order to be able to speak to other people and keep your head held high you much have good self-confidence. This can also extend into the classroom and your child's learning. For example, if your child has very low levels of confidence they will likely be afraid of approaching a teacher and asking for help with what they don't understand. They would rather just take the failing grade because they do not have to interact socially in this way.

Emotional Problems

Long periods of low confidence are likely to cause certain emotional problems. Loss of happiness, anxiety, depression, irritability, and, in extreme cases, suicide are examples of emotional problems. Suicide is most commonly committed by children who believe they are nothing and will never be anything. Sometimes they hide this feeling from their parents, and other times they do not pay enough attention to their parents; either way, it is terrible that a child would do this. All of these emotional issues can have an impact on your child's life now and in the future. That is why, as a parent, it should be your top priority to ensure that your child feels great about themselves and has a high level of self-confidence. Keep in mind all of the negative consequences discussed in this chapter, as well as the fact that there are countless more, and you will undoubtedly be motivated to begin assisting your child in improving their confidence.

Conclusion

In conclusion, your child may be experiencing low levels of self-worth and self-confidence right now, but this does not have to be the case indefinitely. As a parent, you must take the necessary steps to ensure that your child has a bright future full of opportunities. The first step is to ensure that your child feels good about themselves and has healthy levels of self-worth and self-confidence because these are two characteristics that make life's challenges bearable and possible to overcome.

Without the foundation of confidence, your child will most likely be lost when they enter the real world. Without the ability to approach strangers or take on new tasks, even the simplest tasks in life can become a hundred times more difficult. Confidence is more than just a desirable characteristic. To be truly successful in life and to be contempt with themselves, your child must learn to be confident in themselves and to believe in themselves, and you must show them how to do so.

Remember the advice you've learned from this book as you encourage your child to develop their self-confidence; it will be a helpful guide to help you through the process. Additionally, be mindful of the potential consequences if your child doesn't have a healthy level of confidence. I wish you the best of luck and appreciate you reading this book. I hope you enjoyed it and that it will help you in your struggles.